The ABC of educating your pet: Learn to teach them to urinate and defecate without resorting to violence

By Gonzalo Estrada

While every precaution has been taken in the preparation of this book, the publisher assumes no responsibility for errors or omissions, or for damages resulting from the use of the information contained herein.

THE ABC OF EDUCATING YOUR PET

First edition. March 12, 2024.

Copyright © 2024 Gonzalo Estrada.

ISBN: 979-8224197613

Written by Gonzalo Estrada.

Contents

Chapter 1: The Importance of Positive Education

In this chapter, we'll explore why it's essential to use positive, non-violent training methods to educate your pet. The relationship between an owner and their pet is based on trust, love and mutual respect. By educating your pet in a positive way, you not only strengthen these bonds, but you also create an environment conducive to learning and growth.

When we talk about educating a pet, many pet owners adopt the misconception that they can only achieve results through punishment or violence. However, this is not only cruel, but it can also lead to a number of negative consequences. By resorting to violence, pets can experience fear, anxiety and even aggression, which does not contribute to their education or emotional well-being.

On the contrary, positive training methods are based on positive reinforcement and the establishment of clear limits. By rewarding desired behaviors and gently correcting unwanted behaviors, you can teach your pet the right behaviors in an effective and respectful way.

The positive approach is based on the premise that pets learn best through motivation and positive reinforcement. By rewarding them with treats, praise or games when they perform a behavior correctly, we encourage them to repeat it. This gives them a sense of satisfaction and reinforces the connection between stimulus and reward.

In addition, it is important to mention that positive training is not only based on rewarding desired behaviors, but also on ignoring undesirable ones. By not paying attention to them or reacting to inappropriate behavior, we eliminate any benefit or reward they might derive from them, thus discouraging their repetition.

Raising a pet, whether it's a dog, a cat, or any other species, requires patience, consistency and dedication. It is essential to understand that each animal is unique and learns at its own pace. By using positive training methods, you establish a relationship of trust and respect with your pet, which will facilitate their learning and their willingness to follow your instructions.

By educating your pet in a positive way, you're also promoting their emotional and mental well-being. Violence-based training techniques can generate stress, anxiety and fear in the animal, affecting its quality of life in a significant way. On the contrary, positive reinforcement promotes a safe and happy environment, in which your pet can fully develop.

In short, positive education is the key to establishing a harmonious and balanced relationship with your pet. By using training methods based on motivation, positive reinforcement and mutual respect, you give your furry companion the tools they need to learn and grow in a healthy way. In the next part of this chapter, we will delve into specific positive training techniques that you can use with your pet. As we deepen the importance of using positive, non-violent training methods to educate your pet, it is essential to understand the negative consequences that recourse to violence can have. The relationship between you and your pet is unique, and based on trust, love and mutual respect. By educating your pet in a positive way, you not only strengthen these bonds, but you also create an environment conducive to learning and growth.

When owners adopt the misconception that they can only achieve results through punishment or violence, they can have a series of negative consequences for their pet. By resorting to violence, pets can experience fear, anxiety and even aggression, which does not contribute to their education or emotional well-being. In addition, this approach can profoundly damage the trusting relationship you have established with your furry companion.

Instead, positive training methods rely on positive reinforcement and setting clear limits. By rewarding desired behaviors and gently correcting unwanted behaviors, you can teach your pet the right behaviors in an effective and respectful way.

The positive approach is based on the premise that pets learn best through motivation and positive reinforcement. By rewarding them with treats, praise or games when they perform a behavior correctly, we encourage them to repeat it. This gives them a sense of satisfaction and reinforces the connection between stimulus and reward.

However, it is important to note that positive training is not only based on rewarding desired behaviors, but also on ignoring undesirable ones. By not paying attention to them or reacting to inappropriate behavior, we eliminate any benefit or reward they might derive from them, thus discouraging their repetition. This doesn't mean that you completely ignore your pet, but rather that you redirect their attention to appropriate behaviors and reinforce them in a positive way.

Raising a pet, whether it's a dog, a cat, or any other species, requires patience, consistency and dedication. It is essential to understand that each animal is unique and learns at its own pace. By using positive training methods, you establish a relationship of trust and respect with your pet, which will facilitate their learning and their willingness to follow your instructions.

In addition, by educating your pet in a positive way, you are also promoting their emotional and mental well-being. Violence-based training techniques can generate stress, anxiety and fear in the animal, affecting its quality of life in a significant way. On the contrary, positive reinforcement promotes a safe and happy environment, in which your pet can fully develop.

In short, positive education is the key to establishing a harmonious and balanced relationship with your pet. By using training methods based on motivation, positive reinforcement and mutual respect, you give your furry companion the tools they need to learn and grow in a healthy way.

In the next part of this chapter, we'll dive into specific positive training techniques you can use with your pet. We'll explore how to teach him to urinate and defecate without resorting to violent or cruel methods. You will discover that it is possible to educate your pet in an effective and respectful way, building a relationship of trust and lasting love. Keep reading to learn more about the power of positive education in your pet's development.

Chapter 2: Preparing the Right Environment

We will learn how to configure your home environment to facilitate the training of your pet.

When we decide to have a pet, we take responsibility for caring for and educating them in the best possible way. Training is a fundamental aspect to ensure a healthy and harmonious coexistence between us and our faithful companion. In this chapter, we'll focus on the importance of preparing the right environment to facilitate your pet's training process.

The first step in properly configuring the environment is to allocate a specific space for your pet. This space should be comfortable and safe, where your pet feels protected and can rest. You can use a cage, a special bed, or even a designated area in a room in the house. Remember that this space must be exclusive to your pet, avoiding the presence of foreign objects that could distract them or generate stress.

Once you have established the area intended for your pet, it is important to also define the areas where you want it to perform its physiological needs. This can be achieved by using hygienic carpets, newspapers, or even an access door to the outside. The idea is to teach your pet that there are specific places to urinate and defecate, preventing them from doing so anywhere in the house.

Another aspect to consider when preparing the right environment is to maintain good hygiene. Make sure you regularly clean your pet's space, removing waste and eliminating any unpleasant odors. This will help your pet identify the right places for their needs and avoid dirtying other spaces in the home.

In addition to cleaning, it is essential to provide your pet with mental and physical stimulation through toys and activities appropriate to their species. This will help keep her entertained and reduce her anxiety, which in turn will make the training process easier.

It is important to mention that during the training process, it is recommended to establish a daily routine for your pet. This includes specific times to feed him, take him out for a walk and allow him to fulfill his needs. By having an established routine, your pet will be able to anticipate what is expected of it, thus making it easier for them to learn.

In short, preparing the right environment is essential to facilitate the training of your pet. Establishing an exclusive space for her, delimiting suitable areas for urinating and defecating, maintaining good hygiene, providing adequate stimuli and establishing a daily routine are key aspects that will help you educate your pet effectively.

Remember that patience, consistency and understanding are essential qualities when training your pet. In the second part of this chapter, we'll delve into specific techniques to teach your pet to urinate and defecate without resorting to violence. Don't miss it!

(Chapter ends abruptly, without a conclusion) Once you've set up the right environment for your pet, it's time to dive into specific techniques to teach them to urinate and defecate without resorting to violence. Remember that the goal is to educate your pet effectively, using positive and respectful methods.

The first step is to establish clear communication with your pet. Make sure you use short, consistent verbal commands to tell him what you want him to do. For example, you can use "pee" or "poop" clearly and firmly. Accompany these instructions with clear and practical gestures, such as pointing out the designated place or using a specific word such as "bathroom". This will help your pet understand what is expected of them.

A very effective technique for teaching your pet to urinate and defecate in the right place is positive reinforcement. When you see your pet relieving himself in the designated place, praise him and add words of encouragement such as "very well" or "good job". In addition, you can reward her with a small treat or caress so that they associate that behavior with something pleasant. Remember that positive reinforcement is very important to motivate your pet to repeat the appropriate behavior.

It is essential to be patient during this learning process. Your pet may make some mistakes and not learn right away. Instead of resorting to violence or scolding her, focus on redirecting her behavior to the right place. If you catch her in the act, without doing anything violent or aggressive, simply take her calmly to the designated place and use the verbal and gestural commands you've been using. Remember that patience and consistency are key to positive results.

In addition to using positive reinforcement, you can use conditioning techniques. For example, if your pet shows signs that they need to urinate or defecate, quickly get them to the designated place and allow them to relieve themselves. This will help you associate that place with your physiological needs. As your pet learns, you can extend the time between trips to the bathroom, always making sure that it can stay comfortable and without causing any physical discomfort.

Remember that training is not only about teaching your pet to urinate and defecate in the right place, but it also involves establishing a relationship of trust and mutual respect. As you progress through the training process, take the opportunity to strengthen the bond with your pet through fun and loving activities. Play with her, give her attention and affection, and make sure you meet all her basic needs.

In conclusion, training your pet requires an appropriate environment, patience, perseverance and positive techniques. Don't forget that violence has no place in the process of educating your pet. Use respectful methods, positive reinforcement, and clear communication to teach him to urinate and defecate in the right place. Always remember that your pet depends on you for its education and well-being, so enjoy this learning together!

Chapter 3: Getting to Know Your Pet and Establishing Routines

Learn how to better understand your pet's behavior and how to establish effective training routines.

When you decide to bring a pet into your home, be it a dog, a cat or any other animal, it is essential to understand their behavior and establish routines that allow them to adapt in a healthy way to their new environment. In this chapter, we'll explore the importance of getting to know your pet in depth and how to establish training routines. This knowledge and structure are crucial to ensure a harmonious and happy coexistence between you and your faithful companion.

Each pet is unique, with its own characteristics and needs. Therefore, the first step to understanding her is to spend time observing her behavior. Observing how they interact with their environment, how they relate to other animals or people, facial expressions and body postures can provide you with valuable clues about their emotional state and needs. Remember that communication with your pet is not based on words, but on the interpretation of their body language.

Once you understand the signals your pet transmits, you can establish routines that promote their well-being and learning. Routines are essential for animals, as they provide them with safety and stability. Setting fixed times for feeding them, taking them out for walks, playing and resting allows them to anticipate and adapt to daily activities. This not only benefits your pet, but it also makes it easier to train and strengthen the bond between the two.

When it comes to teaching hygiene habits, such as urinating and defecating in the right place, establishing a consistent routine is essential. Constancy and patience will be your allies in this process. Identify the designated area for your pet to relieve himself and bring him to that place at regular intervals. Always cheer her up and reward her with words of praise and a treat when she relieves herself in the right place. This way, you'll associate that behavior with a positive reward and learn to repeat it.

In addition to daily routines, it's important to introduce your pet to new experiences and situations gradually and positively. Exposing her to different sounds, smells or environments from an early age, in a safe environment, will allow her to develop adaptation and confidence skills. However, it is essential to respect your pet's times and limits to avoid generating stressful or traumatic situations.

Remember that each pet is a unique individual, so it is essential to adapt routines and training techniques to their specific characteristics and needs. Not all pets learn the same way or at the same pace, so it's essential to be patient and understanding during the training process.

In short, getting to know your pet in depth and establishing effective routines are fundamental pillars in their education and training. Observing and understanding their body language will allow you to interpret their needs and establish appropriate guidelines for their well-being. Daily routines provide them with security and stability, thus making it easier for them to adapt and learn. Remember to be consistent, patient, and positively reward desired behaviors. In the second part of this chapter, we'll explore additional techniques and tools to improve your pet's training and strengthen your bond. You'll be amazed at what you can achieve together!

(Note: Remember not to include a conclusion or a summary at the end of this first half of the chapter, as we want the suspense to continue for the readers. The second half will follow later.) Once you have established the basic routines for your pet, it's time to delve into additional techniques and tools to perfect their training and strengthen the bond between the two. In this second part of the chapter, we'll explore some useful tips for achieving an effective and successful education.

- Positive reinforcement: One of the most effective techniques for teaching your pet is positive reinforcement. Through this method, you'll reward and reward appropriate and desirable behaviors. You can use treats, verbal praise, or petting as rewards. Remember that positive reinforcement must be immediate and consistent, so that your pet can quickly associate the action with the reward.

- Clicker training: Clicker training is a technique that uses a device called a clicker to mark the desired behavior of your pet. The clicker makes a characteristic sound when pressed, and this sound is associated with a reward. By using the clicker, your pet will learn to associate sound with the right action and will know when they have performed a behavior correctly. This technique is especially useful for teaching more advanced tricks or commands.

- Patience and perseverance: As we mentioned before, each pet is unique and learns at its own pace. It is essential to be patient and consistent during the training process. Don't be discouraged if your pet doesn't learn right away or makes mistakes. Remember that praising and rewarding appropriate behaviors is the key to success in your education.

- Socialization: Early socialization is essential for your pet to learn to relate properly to other animals and people. Exposing her to different environments, noises and situations from an early age will help her develop social skills and feel more comfortable in different situations. Organizing play dates with other dogs, taking her to parks, or walking her in different environments are great ways to socialize your pet.

- Basic obedience training: Teaching your pet basic commands such as "sitting", "still" or "here" is crucial to having adequate control over it. Spend time teaching him these commands using positive reinforcement techniques. Remember to be consistent in your instructions and reward the right behaviors. In addition to providing, you with basic commands, obedience training will also strengthen your bond and improve communication between the two.

- Adapting to new situations: Throughout your pet's life, they are likely to face new and different situations. It's important to help her gradually adapt to these changes, providing her with a safe environment and supporting her emotionally. It can be helpful to use desensitization techniques to help your pet deal with their fears or concerns. Consult an animal behavior professional if you need help in more difficult situations.

In conclusion, your pet's education is not just about teaching them to urinate and defecate in the right place. It's an ongoing process that requires patience, understanding, and dedication on your part. Establishing effective routines, using positive reinforcement techniques, and promoting socialization and adaptability are fundamental aspects of successfully training your pet. Remember that every pet is unique and, as a responsible owner, you must adapt training strategies to their particular needs and characteristics. Enjoy the teaching process and be amazed at what you can achieve together!

Chapter 4: Teaching the right place to urinate and defecate

Learn to teach your pet the right place to do their basic needs without using violence.

In the process of educating our pet, one of the fundamental aspects is to teach them where they should do their basic needs. It is important to note that achieving this learning without resorting to violence is essential to maintaining a relationship of respect and trust with our furry companion.

The first step in teaching your pet the right place to urinate and defecate is to identify a specific area that will serve as their bathroom. It can be a corner of the yard, a tray of sand, or even a space inside the house with a soaker. The important thing is to select a place that is easily accessible to him and that is simple for us to clean.

Once you have chosen the place, you should familiarize your pet with it. You can take him there and allow him to explore the area with peace of mind. You might feel a little confused at first, but this is completely normal. Remember that each pet has its own learning pace, so you must be patient and understanding throughout the process.

The next step is to establish a routine for your pet. Dogs, for example, often need to go out to relieve themselves after eating, drinking water or waking up from a nap. Observe your pet's habits and try to take them to the bathroom at the appropriate times. It is also essential that you do it early in the morning and before going to sleep during the night.

Once you're in the designated area, use consistent verbal commands to tell your pet what you want them to do. You can use phrases like "pee" or "poop" clearly and firmly. Remember that dogs respond more easily to short, direct commands.

It's also important to congratulate your pet every time they relieve themselves correctly in the right place. You can reward him with petting, praise, or even prizes such as special dog treats. This will create a positive association in your mind and reinforce your desired behavior.

It's normal that during the teaching process your pet may make some mistakes and relieve themselves in the wrong places. Faced with this situation, it is essential not to punish him or to resort to violent methods. Violence will only create fear and confusion in your partner, making the learning process even more difficult.

Instead, when you encounter an accident, simply ignore it and clean the area using deodorizing products that remove any trace of odor to prevent your pet from associating it with a suitable place to relieve themselves. Remember that animals have a much more developed sense of smell than ours, so it is essential to ensure deep cleaning.

With perseverance and patience, you'll be able to teach your pet the right place to urinate and defecate. Remember that each pet is a unique individual, so the learning process can take longer in some cases. Do not despair, maintain the constancy and love for your furry companion, and you will eventually achieve the desired results.

Keep reading the next chapter to discover additional techniques to help you improve your pet's education!

The next step in teaching your pet the right place to urinate and defecate is to set clear limits. It's critical for your pet to understand that they should only be relieving themselves in the designated area and not elsewhere in the house or yard. To achieve this, you must be attentive and constantly monitor your pet while it is indoors. If you notice that he begins to show signs that he needs to go to the bathroom, such as sniffing or walking in circles, immediately take him to his designated area.

During this learning stage, your pet may make some mistakes and relieve himself in the wrong places. If this happens, it's important to stay calm and remain firm in your teachings. Never punish him or use violence, as this will only create fear and confusion in your furry companion.

Instead, when you encounter an accident, simply ignore it and clean the area with deodorizing products that remove any trace of odor. Remember that animals have a much more developed sense of smell than ours, so it is essential to ensure deep cleaning.

In addition to setting clear boundaries, you can use positive reinforcement techniques to reinforce the desired behavior in your pet. Every time you relieve yourself in the right place, warmly congratulate him. You can give him cuddles, compliments and even prizes such as special treats for dogs. This will create a positive association in your mind and motivate you to repeat that behavior in the future.

It's important to be consistent and patient during this teaching process. Remember that each pet has its own learning rate, so some may learn faster than others. Maintain consistency and love for your furry companion, and you will eventually achieve the desired results.

If after a considerable time your pet has not yet learned to relieve himself in the right place, it can be useful to consult a professional trainer. They can provide you with additional techniques and strategies to help you with this task.

In conclusion, teaching your pet the right place to urinate and defecate is essential to maintain a harmonious and healthy coexistence. Remember to select a specific area that is easily accessible and easy to clean. Establish a routine to take your pet to the bathroom at the appropriate times and use consistent verbal commands. Use positive reinforcement techniques and remain calm and patient throughout the process. With dedication and perseverance, you will be able to teach your pet to relieve themselves in the right place and build a relationship of respect and trust.

I hope this guide has been useful to you! Remember that each pet is a unique individual, so consider their particular characteristics during the teaching process. Keep learning and discovering new techniques on the next few pages to further improve your pet's education. Continue to provide the love and care your furry companion deserves!

Chapter 5: Using Positive Reinforcement for Training

Learn how to reward your pet in a positive way to motivate their learning and facilitate training.

On the path to educating our pet, it is essential to understand that animals learn best through positive reinforcement, that is, by rewarding desirable behaviors. Although it seems obvious, violence or coercive training methods are practices that we must avoid at all costs. In this chapter, you'll learn how to use positive reinforcement effectively to help your pet learn to urinate and defecate properly without resorting to violence.

Positive reinforcement can be anything the pet finds enjoyable and wants to get. It can be a small treat, a word of praise, or even a fun game. The key is to find the reward that best motivates your pet. Every animal is different and what may work for one, may not work for another. Therefore, it's important to watch your pet carefully and understand what stimuli generate the most enthusiasm.

When starting training, you must be patient and start with realistic goals. Divide the process into small steps and with each achievement, reward your pet in a positive way. You can use clicker training, a technique that involves associating a sound (the click of the clicker) with obtaining the reward. This will allow your pet to associate sound with behavior and to effectively reinforce it.

Remember that the time to reward is key. You should always do this right away, so that the pet clearly identifies what behavior has been rewarded. In addition, use clear and concise language to indicate good behavior, so the pet can quickly associate the desired action with the reward.

During training, it is important to avoid overcompensation. That is, we should not reward our pet for behaviors that are not related to the objective of the training. Excessive reinforcement can confuse our pet and make it difficult to learn the desired behaviors.

Another important aspect is consistency. You must maintain the same way of reinforcing positive behaviors at all times. If you ever don't reward the desired action, you'll be sending a confusing message to your pet and you may not get the expected results.

Using rewards in training not only motivates your pet, it also helps to strengthen the bond between the two. Positive reinforcement creates an environment of trust and affection, where the pet feels valued and part of the family.

In short, the use of positive reinforcement in training your pet is essential to achieve desirable behaviors without resorting to violence. By rewarding appropriately and consistently, you'll motivate your pet to learn and to actively participate in their own training. In the second part of this chapter, we will discover advanced techniques to reinforce learning and overcome common difficulties during the educational process. Get ready to keep learning and be surprised with the results! During the second part of this chapter, we will delve into more advanced techniques to reinforce your pet's learning and overcome common difficulties that may arise during the educational process. Get ready to keep learning and be surprised with the results!

A very effective technique for training your pet is modeling, which consists of using concrete examples to teach it the desired behavior. You can use other trained dogs or even online videos as references to show your pet how to properly perform its physiological needs. Modeling can be a powerful tool for teaching your pet to urinate and defecate in the right place, as long as you combine it with positive reinforcement.

Another useful technique is training time management. It's important to remember that pets have limited attention spans, so short, frequent sessions are often more effective than long, infrequent sessions. Take a few minutes several times a day to work on training your pet, making sure that both you and your pet are relaxed and free of distractions.

During the training process, your pet may make mistakes or fail to perform the desired behavior right away. It's critical to maintain patience and consistency at this time. If your pet makes a mistake, don't scold them, just ignore the bad behavior and reinforce the right behavior again. For the process to be effective, it's important that your pet clearly associates the reward with the right behavior, so they can learn from their mistakes and gradually improve.

Remember that training a pet isn't just limited to inside the home. When you go out for walks with your pet, take the opportunity to reinforce desired behaviors, such as urinating and defecating in the right places. Take small treats or rewards with you to reward your pet when it performs its needs correctly outside the home. In this way, your pet will associate the prize with specific behavior, making it easier for them to learn and strengthen their connection with you.

During the training process, it's also important to consider your pet's individual needs. Some dogs may have difficulty controlling their needs due to health problems, stress, or anxiety. If you notice that your pet has persistent difficulties learning to urinate and defecate in the right place, it is advisable to consult a veterinarian or professional trainer. They can help you identify the possible causes of problems and offer you specific strategies to address them.

In conclusion, using positive reinforcement and advanced training techniques can be really effective in teaching your pet to urinate and defecate without resorting to violence. Remember that every pet is unique and may require different approaches, so it's important to be flexible and adapt to the individual needs of your furry companion.

With patience, consistency and positive reinforcement, you can help your pet learn effectively and strengthen the special bond that unites them. Keep practicing and enjoy the learning process with your pet!

Chapter 6: Establishing feeding and walking schedules

L earn how to establish feeding and walking routines to contribute to your pet's successful training.

The key to effective pet education is based on consistency and established routines. Establishing feeding and walking schedules for your pet will not only help to maintain their health and well-being, but it will also facilitate the training process. In this chapter, you'll learn how to effectively establish these routines.

Let's start by talking about feeding schedules. It's important to establish a regular schedule to provide your pet with their daily meals. By doing so, you'll be teaching your pet to be disciplined and to understand that food will be provided at specific times. In addition, by having fixed feeding schedules, you can better control the amount of food your pet consumes, thus avoiding problems of overweight or obesity.

To establish an appropriate feeding schedule, you need to consider your pet's individual needs. Some breeds or sizes of dogs, for example, may require more food than others. Consult your veterinarian to determine the appropriate amount of food and the frequency of meals based on your pet's age, weight, and activity level.

Once you've defined your portions and meal frequencies, it's important to keep your schedules consistent. Try to feed your pet at the same time every day. This will help establish a routine and teach your pet to wait patiently for their food. Remember that it's important that you don't offer extra food between scheduled meals, as this could interfere with their ability to follow set times.

Let's now move on to talking about walking schedules. As with food, it's important to establish a routine for your pet's walks. Dogs, in particular, need regular opportunities to exercise, explore their environment, and meet their physiological needs.

Determining the frequency and duration of walks will again depend on your pet's individual needs. Some dogs will need longer, more frequent walks, while others might be satisfied with shorter walks. Your pet's breed, age, energy level, and health are important factors to consider. Also, make sure you always carry bags to collect your pet's feces to keep your neighborhood clean and safe.

To establish an effective walking routine, try to take your pet out at the same time every day. This will allow your pet to anticipate and look forward to that moment. Also, make sure you give her plenty of time to explore and meet her physiological needs during walks.

In short, establishing regular feeding and walking schedules for your pet is essential to the success of their training. Consistency in these routines will help your pet understand expectations and develop discipline. Remember to check with your veterinarian to determine your pet's individual needs and adjust schedules accordingly.

In the second half of this chapter, we'll continue to explore how to make the most of these feeding schedules and walks to train your pet. Don't miss it! Let's continue to learn how to establish effective feeding and walking schedules for your pet's successful training!

Once you've established your eating schedules, it's important to follow them consistently. Avoid offering additional food between scheduled meals, as this can interfere with your pet's ability to follow set times. Remember that the goal of establishing regular feeding schedules is to teach your pet discipline and patience. By having a consistent routine, your pet will learn to wait patiently for their food and you will avoid behavioral problems related to feeding.

In addition to establishing feeding schedules, it is also essential to establish a routine for your pet's walks. Walks are not only important for your pet to exercise and explore their environment, but also to meet their physiological needs.

When determining the frequency and duration of walks, consider your pet's individual needs. Depending on their breed, age, energy level, and health, some dogs will need longer, more frequent walks than others. Be sure to adapt the walks to the specific characteristics and needs of your pet.

To establish an effective walking routine, try to take your pet out at the same time every day. This will help your pet anticipate and look forward to that moment, making training easier. During walks, it's also important to make sure you give him enough time to meet his physiological needs and explore his environment.

Remember to always carry bags to collect your pet's faces during walks. This is essential to keeping the neighborhood clean and safe, and demonstrates your responsibility as a pet owner.

In short, establishing regular feeding and walking schedules for your pet is essential for their training and overall well-being. Consistency in these routines will help your pet understand expectations and develop discipline. Remember to adapt schedules and routines to your pet's individual needs, and don't forget to check with your veterinarian for specific recommendations.

By following these tips, you'll be on the right path to establishing effective feeding and walking routines to aid in your pet's education. Remember that training requires time, patience and dedication, but the results will be worth it.

Keep practicing and giving your pet the love and care it deserves! Good luck on your training journey together!

Chapter 7: Overcoming Common Obstacles and Mistakes

Identify the most common training mistakes and learn how to overcome them to achieve success with your pet.

Training a pet can be a rewarding but also a challenging process. Sometimes, we run into obstacles and make mistakes in the process. However, it is important to remember that patience and consistency are key to getting our pet to learn to urinate and defecate in the right place without resorting to violence. In this chapter, we'll explore the most common mistakes that can arise during training and how to overcome them.

One of the most common mistakes is a lack of consistency. Often, we make the mistake of being inconsistent with the rules and expectations we set for our pet. It's important to remember that dogs, for example, are animals of habit and need a clear routine to understand what's expected of them. If we constantly change the rules or areas designated to relieve themselves, we will confuse our pet and hinder their learning process.

Another common mistake is a lack of patience. Understanding and accepting that the training process takes time is essential. It's important to remember that every pet has its own learning pace. Some will be able to learn quickly, while others may need more time. Patience and perseverance are key to overcoming this obstacle and to avoid resorting to violent methods.

A mistake related to patience is to punish our pet for accidents. It's crucial to understand that accidents can happen, especially during the early stages of training. Scolding or physically punishing our pet for an accident will only cause fear and confusion in it. Instead, we must focus on positively reinforcing appropriate behaviors and calmly and consistently correcting errors.

Another common obstacle is a lack of understanding of our pet's signs. Every pet has subtle ways of communicating with us and we must learn to read those signs. Observing their body language and behaviors will help us understand when they need to go to the bathroom and avoid accidents. Paying attention to our pet's signs will allow us to anticipate their needs and respond appropriately.

It can also be difficult to overcome the obstacles associated with caring for and cleaning the areas where our pet is relieving itself. It is important to keep in mind that we must offer an adequate and clean space so that our pet feels comfortable and motivated to use it. The lack of cleanliness or the presence of strong odors in the area can hinder the training process. Let's make sure to keep the areas clean and eliminate any residual odors to encourage our pet's learning success.

In short, training our pet can present common challenges and mistakes. However, by identifying and addressing them with patience, consistency and understanding, we can overcome them and achieve success in the process of teaching them to urinate and defecate without resorting to violence. In the second part of this chapter, we'll explore additional strategies and tips for successfully overcoming these obstacles. Don't miss the next installment!

Continuation of Chapter 7: Overcoming Common Obstacles and Mistakes

In the first part of this chapter, we identified some of the most common mistakes we can make while training our pet to learn to urinate and defecate in the right place without resorting to violence. Now, we'll continue to explore additional strategies and tips to successfully overcome these obstacles.

A mistake that is often made is not demonstrating clarity in instructions. It is essential to be clear and consistent in the instructions we give to our pet. Using simple words and clear commands, together with gestures or visual cues, will make it easier for our pet to understand. In addition, it is important to immediately and consistently reward appropriate behaviors, to positively reinforce their learning.

It is also essential to be realistic about the expectations we have for our pet. Every animal is different, and some may need more time and effort to learn certain behaviors. Not all dogs, cats or other pets will adapt to training in the same way, so it's important to be patient and adapt techniques to the individual needs of our pet.

Another common obstacle is a lack of commitment and consistency on the part of pet owners. Training is not only about teaching our pet to urinate and defecate in the right place, but also about establishing a relationship of trust and mutual respect. Therefore, it is essential to make training a constant part of our daily routine, dedicating regular time and effort to reinforcing the desired rules and behaviors.

Distraction is another mistake we must avoid. During the training process, it is important to eliminate any distractions that may hinder our pet's learning. Turning off the television, avoiding excessive noise or keeping other pets away during training sessions will help us keep our pet focused and make it easier for them to understand what is expected of them.

Another important strategy for overcoming obstacles in training is to establish a clear and consistent routine. Pets feel more secure and confident when they have an established routine, giving them a sense of predictability and control. Establishing regular times for feeding, taking out for a walk and allowing our pet to relieve themselves will greatly contribute to their learning success.

Finally, we must always remember to positively reinforce appropriate behaviors and avoid physically punishing our pet. Positive reinforcement, such as prizes, caresses or words of encouragement, has a much longer lasting and effective impact on our pet's learning and behavior. Using negative reinforcement or punishment will only generate fear and stress, which can hinder her learning process and weaken our relationship with her.

In conclusion, overcoming common obstacles and mistakes in training our pet will require patience, consistency and understanding. Identifying and addressing these errors will allow us to succeed in the process of teaching them to urinate and defecate without resorting to violence. Remember to be clear in your instructions, be realistic in your expectations, show commitment and consistency, avoid distractions, establish clear routines, and positively reinforce appropriate behaviors. Don't miss out on the additional tools and tips we'll present in the following chapters to help you achieve a successful education for your pet!

Chapter 8: The Power of Patience and Consistency

Learn how patience and consistency are essential to educating your pet effectively and without violence.

Raising a pet can be a challenge, but with patience and consistency, a harmonious and respectful coexistence can be achieved. Like humans, pets need time to learn and adapt to the norms and expectations of their environment. In this chapter, we'll explore the power of patience and consistency in your pet's education process.

Patience is a virtue that we must cultivate when educating our pets. Sometimes, we find ourselves wanting quick results and become impatient when our pet doesn't immediately understand or obey. However, it's important to remember that every pet is different and learns at their own pace. Just as you can't expect a child to learn to walk from one day to the next, neither can we expect our pet to learn all the commands and behaviors instantly.

Patience during the education process is critical. Sometimes your pet may not follow the instructions correctly or may be easily distracted. At such times, you need to remember that patience and perseverance are key. Instead of losing patience, try to positively reinforce the desired behavior and redirect your attention when you become distracted. Remember that the goal is to teach them in a loving and non-violent way.

Consistency is another fundamental pillar in your pet's education. Pets need to establish routines and learn through repetition. If you use a different technique or approach every day, your pet is likely to become confused and unable to understand what is expected of it. For this reason, it's essential to set clear rules and maintain consistency in how you teach and correct their behavior.

By being consistent, we are providing our pet with a predictable structure and environment in which to learn and grow. This provides them with security and confidence, which is essential for their emotional well-being. Remember that pets seek approval and love from their owners, and by being consistent in our teaching, we are providing them with clear guidance and establishing a stronger connection with them.

Patience and consistency go hand in hand in the process of educating your pet. Patience allows us to accept that learning takes time and that we must have realistic expectations. Meanwhile, consistency helps us to maintain a clear structure and to convey to our pet what is expected of it in a coherent way.

By combining these two elements, we will be creating an optimal environment for the education and development of our pet. With patience and consistency, we can achieve lasting results and build a relationship based on mutual respect and trust.

In the next chapter, we'll explore various techniques and strategies to effectively apply patience and consistency to your pet's education. Get ready to discover powerful tools that will help you strengthen the bond with your furry companion!

Patience and consistency are crucial elements in your pet's education process, and in this second half of the chapter, we'll explore some specific techniques and strategies to effectively apply these principles.

One of the most important strategies for teaching your pet consistently is to establish clear rules and be consistent in their application. This involves maintaining a daily routine and using the same words and commands for each behavior you want to teach him. For example, if you're teaching your dog to sit, always use the same word and gesture to tell him to sit down. This will help your pet associate the word with the action and, over time, understand it better.

Another effective technique is to positively reinforce the desired behavior. Instead of punishing or scolding your pet for unwanted behavior, focus on rewarding and praising their right actions. You can use treats, cuddles, verbal praise, or games as rewards. This positively reinforces the behavior you want to encourage and encourages your pet to repeat it in the future.

It's important to remember that positive reinforcement must be immediate, that is, rewarding your pet as soon as it performs the desired behavior. This way, your pet will associate the reward with its specific action and will have a better understanding of what is expected of it.

Consistency also involves correcting unwanted behavior consistently and without violence. If your pet makes a mistake or doesn't follow an order, it's important to correct it firmly but calmly. For example, if your cat scratches a piece of furniture, you can firmly say "no" and redirect their attention to an appropriate scratcher. Avoid scolding her excessively or using physical punishment, as this can create fear or anxiety in your pet.

Remember that learning your pet takes time and requires patience. You may not get immediate results at first, but persevere and continue to apply the techniques consistently. Every pet is unique and learns at its own pace.

Another important aspect to consider is empathy for your pet. Putting yourself in their shoes will help you better understand their needs and understand why they act a certain way. For example, if your dog pulls on the leash during walks, try to understand if this is due to his excess energy or his curiosity to explore the environment. Once you understand their motivations, you'll be able to address the behavior more effectively.

In short, patience and consistency are fundamental pillars in your pet's education. Through clear rules, positive reinforcement, coherent corrections and empathy, you can establish a relationship based on respect and mutual trust. Remember that every pet is unique and will learn at its own pace, so it's worth adapting education strategies to the individual needs of your furry companion.

In the next chapter, we'll dive into the world of advanced techniques and strategies to continue strengthening the bond with your pet. Don't miss it!

Chapter 9: Dealing with Stressful Situations During Training

Learn to identify and manage stressful situations during your pet's training to avoid any aggressive behavior.

The education and training of our pets can be rewarding moments, full of joy and satisfaction. However, sometimes, certain stressful situations can arise during the teaching process, which can lead to aggressive behavior on the part of our beloved pet. This is why it is essential to learn to identify, manage and prevent these situations, thus maintaining a safe and harmonious environment for all.

The first thing to understand is that animals can also experience stressful situations, just like human beings. Stress can manifest itself in a variety of ways, such as excessive barking, panting, tremors, attempts to flee, among other behaviors that indicate discomfort or fear in our pet. You need to pay attention to these signs in order to act accordingly.

One of the main factors that can cause stress for our pet's during training is the lack of patience and understanding on our part. It is important to remember that each animal has its own learning rate and that we must be patient and respectful with it. Pressuring or forcing our pet will only increase their stress level and make the training process even more difficult.

Another stressful situation for our pets can be the introduction of new stimuli during training. For example, if we are teaching our dog to relieve himself in a specific place, the presence of other animals or unknown people could generate anxiety and discomfort. It's essential to provide a calm, distraction-free environment so that they can concentrate and learn effectively.

In addition, it's critical to understand that every pet has their own stress triggers. It can be the noise of cars, firecrackers or even visits to the vet. By knowing what these triggers are, we can anticipate and adopt preventive measures to minimize their impact on training.

An effective strategy for dealing with stressful situations during training is the use of desensitization and counterconditioning techniques. These techniques involve gradually exposing our pet to stress-causing stimuli, in a controlled and positive way. For example, if our dog is stressed by loud noises, we can start by exposing him to a soft and pleasant sound, while rewarding him with prizes and praise. Little by little, we will increase the intensity of the sound, always positively reinforcing their calm behavior. This will help our pet associate stressful stimuli with positive experiences, thus reducing their level of anxiety.

It is important to note that the emotional well-being of our pet is essential during training. We must ensure that we provide them with sufficient rest time and adequate physical activity, as this will contribute to reducing stress and maintaining a balanced behavior. In addition, positive reinforcement, such as praise, caresses and prizes, is a very effective tool to motivate our pet and reinforce desired behaviors during training.

In short, training our pet can face us in stressful situations. However, by identifying such situations and handling them appropriately, we can avoid any manifestations of aggressiveness. Remember to be patient, understanding and adapt training to your pet's needs and learning pace. In the second half of this chapter, we will discuss additional strategies for managing stressful situations and further improving the training process. Keep reading and discover how to achieve a successful and harmonious training with your beloved pet! During the training of our pet, it is common to encounter additional stress situations that we must handle properly to ensure a successful and smooth process. In this second half of the chapter, we'll explore additional strategies and techniques for dealing with these situations and promoting a safe, positive, and harmonious training environment.

One of the most common stress situations during pet training is the inability to quickly learn certain commands or actions. It is important to remember that each animal has its own learning process and that some may need more time than others to understand and assimilate the lessons. We shouldn't be discouraged or frustrated if our pets don't immediately respond to our teachings. Instead, we must be patient, persistent and positively reinforce the progress and achievements they make.

Another stressful situation that can arise during training is the use of physical punishment or correction. It is essential to avoid any form of violence or abuse towards our pets, as this not only generates stress and fear, but it can also damage the relationship of trust we have built with them. Instead, we should focus on positive reinforcement and praise and reward desired behaviors. Remember that love and patience are the basis of effective and respectful training.

In the case of dogs, a stressful situation that can arise during training is socialization with other dogs. Some pets may feel uncomfortable or fearful when they encounter other dogs, which can make the training process difficult. It is important to approach this situation gradually, exposing our pet to other dogs in a controlled and positive way. Organizing encounters with friendly, well-trained dogs in safe, supervised environments can help reduce stress and encourage positive, balanced interaction.

In addition, it is essential to note that some stressful situations can be triggered by previous negative experiences. If our pet has had bad experiences in the past, such as being abandoned or abused, it is likely that they have developed fears and traumas that affect their learning process. In these cases, it's critical to provide them with a safe environment full of patience and understanding. As our pet feels more secure and confident, they will be able to advance their training more effectively.

To help reduce stress during training, we can also use relaxation and calming techniques, such as deep breathing and gentle massage. These techniques can help your pet relax and concentrate on learning, instead of focusing on stressful situations. It is important to dedicate time to these activities before and after training, to promote relaxation and emotional well-being for our pet.

In conclusion, the training of our pet can present stressful situations that we must handle with care to avoid any aggressive behavior. Let's remember to be patient, persistent and respectful of our pet's learning pace. Let's avoid the use of physical punishment and prioritize positive reinforcement and the creation of a safe and distraction-free environment. By implementing these additional strategies and techniques, we can continue to promote successful, harmonious and loving training with our beloved pets.

Chapter 10: Facing Fear and Anxiety

Explore techniques to help your pet overcome fear and anxiety related to elimination training.

Fear and anxiety can affect our pets in a variety of ways. Some dogs and cats may experience fear when taught to urinate and defecate in specific places, which can hinder the elimination training process. Fortunately, there are effective techniques we can apply to help our pets overcome these fears and anxieties.

First, it's important to understand that every pet is unique and may have different triggers for their fear and anxiety. Some animals may be afraid of certain sounds, smells, or situations that are associated with the elimination process. Identifying these triggers is critical to addressing the problem.

One technique that may be useful is desensitization. It consists of gradually exposing the pet to the triggers of their fear or anxiety in a controlled and positive way. For example, if your dog is scared by the sound of the toilet, you can start by turning it on at a distance where it doesn't make him afraid. Over time and with patience, approach it little by little until you feel more comfortable and relaxed. By reinforcing this process with rewards and petting, your pet will gradually associate the experience with something positive.

Another useful technique is counterconditioning. It consists of systematically associating fear or anxiety with something pleasant or positive. For example, if your cat gets stressed using the litter box, you can reward him with a treat or a pet every time he approaches or enters the box. In this way, the cat will begin to associate the litter box with a pleasant experience and reduce its anxiety.

In addition to these techniques, it's important to create a calm and safe environment for our pets during elimination training. Avoiding loud noises, providing them with a comfortable place to relieve themselves, and showing them calm and patience will be key to their emotional well-being during this process.

It's essential to remember that every pet has their own learning rate and that overcoming fear and anxiety can take time. Don't despair if you don't see immediate results, remember that your patience and perseverance are key to the success of this process.

In the second part of this chapter, we'll explore additional techniques to help our pets deal with fear and anxiety related to elimination training. We'll discover how to build trust in our pets, manage stressful situations and strengthen the bond between us and our furry companions.

Don't miss the continuation of this chapter, where we'll delve into effective strategies for overcoming fear and anxiety in elimination training!

In the second part of this chapter, we will continue to explore additional techniques to help our pets cope with fear and anxiety related to elimination training. Focusing on building trust in our pets, managing stressful situations and strengthening the bond between us and our furry companions.

An effective technique to help our dogs and cats overcome fear and anxiety is positive reinforcement. This technique consists of rewarding and praising our pet every time it performs a desired behavior during the elimination process. For example, when your dog urinates or poops in the designated place, you can praise him and give him a treat as a reward. This will help associate the act of eliminating in the right place with something positive, promoting your confidence and reducing anxiety.

In addition to positive reinforcement, it's important to provide our pets with a safe and comfortable environment during elimination training. This means keeping designated places clean so they can relieve themselves, making sure they have access to fresh water, and providing them with the opportunity to exercise regularly. A healthy and stimulating environment will help reduce stress and anxiety in our pets.

In cases of more serious fear and anxiety, it may be helpful to seek the help of an animal behavior professional. The trainer or veterinarian will be able to assess the situation and provide specific recommendations to address the problem. They can teach you more advanced and personalized techniques that adapt to your pet's needs.

Another fundamental aspect of helping our pets cope with fear and anxiety is to properly manage stressful situations.

We must avoid punishing or scolding our pet when it makes mistakes during the elimination training process. Instead, we must remain calm and redirect their attention to the right behavior. This will help to avoid negative associations with the act of eliminating and to strengthen the bond between us and our pet.

In addition, it is important to highlight the importance of patience and consistency during this process. Each pet has its own learning rate, so it's essential to remember that the results won't be immediate. Don't despair if your pet makes mistakes or shows emotional resilience. Stay consistent in applying training techniques and keep a positive attitude. With time and perseverance, you can help your pet overcome the fear and anxiety related to elimination training.

In short, fear and anxiety can have a significant impact on the elimination training process for our pets. However, there are effective techniques we can implement to help them overcome these challenges. From desensitization and counterconditioning to positive reinforcement and the proper management of stressful situations, we have powerful tools to support our pets in this important learning process. Don't forget that every pet is unique and that time, patience and consistency are key to their success. Go ahead and help your pet overcome their fears and anxieties so they can enjoy a happy and healthy life with you!

Chapter 11: The Importance of Socialization in Training

Understand the importance of socialization for your pet's effective training and how to implement it properly.

Socialization is a fundamental part of the education of our pets. Not only does it contribute to their healthy development, but it also facilitates the training process and strengthens the bond between the owner and the animal. In this chapter, we'll explore the importance of socialization and how to successfully incorporate it into your little companion's training.

Socialization refers to the process of familiarizing our pet with different situations, environments, people and other animals. The goal is to help them adapt and behave appropriately in a variety of circumstances. By exposing them to different stimuli from an early age, animals learn to control their fear, anxiety and aggression, and to respond positively.

Good early socialization is especially important for puppies. During the first weeks of life, puppies are very receptive and tend to learn quickly, making it easier for them to adapt to new experiences. Exposing them to different sounds, smells, people and animals during this crucial period will ensure that they develop a confident and friendly attitude towards their environment.

To implement successful socialization, we must gradually expose our pet to different situations. Start by introducing them to family members and close friends, making sure they are calm and respectful to the animal.

Then, move on to encounters in public spaces where you can interact with other people and animals in a controlled manner.

It's critical to monitor these interactions and ensure that, they are positive. If you notice signs of discomfort or tension in your pet, it's important to step in and provide support. Do not force situations that can generate stress or fear, as this can have the opposite effect to the desired one and generate a negative response in your pet.

Remember that socialization isn't just limited to encounters with people and other animals. It's also important to expose your pet to different environments and stimuli. Walking on the street, visiting parks, slowly introduce new sounds and objects, such as vacuums, hairdryers or rockets. These experiences will enrich your world and help you to adapt to various scenarios in a calm and confident manner.

It is essential to keep in mind that socialization must be an ongoing process. This is not just an initial stage, but a constant practice throughout the life of our pet. New experiences and encounters can continue to enrich their behavior and improve their ability to adapt to different situations.

In conclusion, socialization is a key pillar in the effective training of our pet. Through it, we can help them develop positive behavior, improve their ability to adapt and strengthen our bond with them. Early and gradual socialization, along with careful supervision, will ensure that our pet grows up in a balanced and happy environment. In the second part of this chapter, we'll explore how to address common challenges in socialization and provide practical advice for successful implementation. The importance of socialization in training our pets extends beyond the initial stage of their lives. As they grow, they continue to need positive experiences and contact with different people and situations to keep their behavior balanced and adapt to changes in their environment. In this second part of the chapter, we'll explore some common challenges that can arise during socialization and provide practical advice to overcome them.

One of the most common challenges in pet socialization is aggression towards other dogs or animals. It's important to remember that aggression is not a natural reaction for dogs, but is generally a response learned through previous negative experiences. If your pet shows signs of aggression during encounters with other animals, it's critical to address the problem appropriately. The ideal is to seek the help of a professional pet trainer, who can provide you with specific techniques and strategies to correct this unwanted behavior.

Another common challenge in socialization is separation anxiety. Many dogs experience distress or stress when left home alone, which can result in destructive behavior or excessive vocalizations. To address this problem, it's essential to start with proper socialization from an early age. Be sure to gradually expose your pet to being alone, starting with short periods and gradually increasing the duration. In addition, providing them with interactive toys or food puzzles can keep them busy and distracted while they are alone.

The lack of socialization with certain stimuli can lead to our pets' developing fears or phobias. It's important to gradually introduce different sounds and objects into their environment so that they get used to them and don't see them as threats. For example, you can use recordings of firecrackers or fireworks sounds to familiarize your pet with these noises before having a real experience. Always remember to associate these stimuli with something positive, such as prizes or games, to reinforce a positive response.

Effective communication with our pet also plays a key role in the socialization process. Learning to interpret their body language and stress signals will help us identify situations that may cause discomfort or fear. For example, if your dog shows signs of tension, such as bristling his hair or keeping his tail between his hind legs, it's important to intervene calmly and provide him with safety. Make sure you don't punish or scold him, as this will only increase his anxiety and make the situation worse.

In addition to addressing common challenges in socialization, it is also essential to continue providing new and positive experiences to our pet throughout their lives. This includes continuing controlled encounters with people and animals, as well as exposing them to different environments and stimuli. Maintaining a regular socialization program will help keep your confidence and behavior balanced.

In short, proper socialization is a fundamental factor in the education of our pets. Through gradual and positive exposure to different situations, people and animals, we can help them develop appropriate behavior and strengthen our bond with them. As we face common challenges related to socialization, let's remember that patience and persistence are key to overcoming them. By providing continuous socialization throughout our pet's life, we will be ensuring a balanced and happy environment for them.

Continue to practice socialization with your pet and enjoy the benefits of having a trusting company adapted to different situations!

Chapter 12: Maintaining Proper Hygiene and Care

Learn to maintain good hygiene and care for your pet to ensure continued training success. Your furry companion deserves a clean and safe environment, and it's your responsibility to provide him with the necessary care. In this chapter, we are going to discuss some fundamental aspects of keeping your pet clean and healthy.

Your pet's hygiene starts from the inside out. Adequate nutrition is essential to keep your skin and coat in optimal condition. Make sure you provide her with a balanced, quality diet that contains all the essential nutrients for her well-being. Shiny hair and smooth skin are indicators of good nutrition.

In addition to food, regular brushing is also vital to your pet's health. Depending on the breed, the type of hair and the length of the hair, you'll need to establish an appropriate brushing routine. This habit not only eliminates dead hair and knots, but it also stimulates the production of natural oils in the skin, promoting a healthy and shiny coat.

We can't forget the importance of regular baths. However, it's vital to use specific pet products, as human products can be harmful to their sensitive skin. Make sure you choose a shampoo that's right for your coat type and breed. Remember not to bathe him too much, as this could lead to imbalances in the production of natural oils.

Another fundamental aspect of your pet's hygiene is the care of their ears and teeth. Dogs and cats can be prone to infections if they are not given enough attention. Clean your ears regularly with products recommended by your veterinarian and regularly check your pet's oral health. Dental care includes brushing your teeth, but it can also be complemented by specific toys or other products recommended by a professional.

Last but not least, it's essential to keep the space where your pet lives clean. This involves regularly cleaning your bed, toys, and any other area you have access to. Use safe, non-toxic disinfectant products to ensure the elimination of bacteria and germs. If your pet is relieving itself indoors, it's vital to pick up and clean immediately to avoid contamination and bad odors.

In conclusion, maintaining good hygiene and proper care is essential to your pet's well-being and health. A good diet, regular brushing, proper baths, and ear and tooth care are just a few things to consider. Don't forget to keep your environment clean, providing a safe and healthy space for your furry companion. By following these tips, you'll ensure continued training success and promote a happy and healthy life for your pet.

(Without concluding this first part of the chapter, we will now delve into other important aspects for the care and hygiene of your pet. We'll discover additional recommendations and practical tips to help you keep your furry companion in top condition. Let's continue to explore these vital areas of care to ensure the happiness and well-being of our beloved pets!) In the second half of this chapter, we'll focus on other important aspects of maintaining proper hygiene and care for your pet. We'll continue to provide you with additional recommendations and practical advice to help you ensure the well-being of your furry companion.

Nail care is essential to your pet's health and comfort. Long nails can cause pain when walking and even deform your pets' fingers. It is recommended that you check and trim your dog's or cat's nails regularly. If you don't feel comfortable doing it yourself, you can turn to a vet or dog grooming professional to do it for you.

In addition, it's essential to keep your pet protected against fleas, ticks and other parasites. These can cause illness and discomfort for your furry companion. Consult your veterinarian for recommendations on the best antiparasitic products for your pet. Remember to apply these products according to the manufacturer's instructions and regularly monitor for any signs of parasites.

It's also important to pay attention to the temperature of the environment where your pet lives. Make sure it's adequately protected in cold weather and avoid being overexposed to heat during the summer. Keep in mind that some dog and cat breeds are more sensitive to extreme temperatures, so it's essential to provide them with a comfortable and safe environment all year round.

Regular exercise is essential to keeping your pet in good physical and mental shape. Make sure he gets enough daily activity, whether through walks, games, or training sessions. Proper exercise not only helps maintain a healthy weight, it also helps prevent behavioral problems and stimulates your pet's mind.

In addition, we must not forget the importance of regular checkups with the vet. These visits are opportunities for your pet's health professional to assess their general condition, identify any health problems, and administer necessary vaccines. Be sure to keep your vaccinations and routine visits up to date to ensure the long-term health of your furry companion.

Last but not least, it's essential to provide your pet with love, attention and companionship. Spending quality time with your furry companion will strengthen the bond between you and promote your emotional well-being. Make sure you dedicate time every day to playing, petting and paying attention to your pet. This will provide them with happiness and security.

In conclusion, by maintaining good hygiene and proper care, you ensure the well-being and health of your pet. Take care of your nails, protect them from parasites, maintain the right temperature in their environment, provide regular exercise, and don't forget to visit the vet. Also, provide love and companionship to promote their emotional well-being. By following these tips, you'll be providing a clean and safe environment for your pet, and ensuring their continued happiness and well-being.

I hope you find these tips helpful in keeping your pet happy and healthy. Continue exploring the ABCs of educating your pet to learn more about how to develop and strengthen your relationship with your furry companion!

Chapter 13: Reinforcing Long-Term Training

Learn how to continue strengthening your pet's training even after you've achieved your initial goals.

Once your pet has learned to urinate and defecate in the designated place without resorting to violence, it's important to maintain training to ensure long-term results. In this chapter, we'll explore some additional strategies to help you consolidate your furry companion's learning.

One of the keys to reinforcing long-term training is consistency. It is essential that you continue to apply the same techniques and commands used during the initial training. This will help your pet remember and reinforce desired behaviors. In addition, we recommend that you establish a daily routine to take your pet to their designated area to relieve themselves. Consistency and repetition are fundamental pillars in the animals' learning process.

Another important aspect of long-term training is patience. Even if your pet has learned to urinate and defecate in the right place, there may occasionally be regressions in behavior. This can happen because of changes in your environment, stress, or even because of illness. In the face of these setbacks, it's essential to stay calm and re-reinforce your training from the start if necessary.

A widely used technique to strengthen pet training is positive reinforcement. This involves rewarding your furry companion every time they correctly perform the desired behavior. You can use treats, verbal praise, or petting as rewards. Remember that positive reinforcement is most effective when it's given immediately after your pet has done what you asked for. This will help you associate the specific action with the reward and reinforce your learning.

In addition to positive reinforcement, it's important to avoid physical or emotional punishment during the long-term training reinforcement process. The use of violence will only create fear and stress in your pet, which can lead to a decline in their training. Remember that the main objective is to establish a relationship of trust and mutual respect.

Another strategy you can use to strengthen your training is to incorporate exercises and games that stimulate the desired behavior. For example, you can play fetch with your pet after they have relieved themselves in the right place. This positively reinforces your action and gives you additional stimulus, thus strengthening learning.

Remember that every pet is unique and may respond differently to the reinforcement of long-term training. See how your furry companion behaves and adapts techniques according to their needs and preferences. If you notice your pet starting to regress in their training, don't be discouraged. It persists patiently and constantly reinforces learning.

In short, to strengthen your pet's training in the long term, you must apply consistent strategies, be patient, use positive reinforcement, and avoid any form of violence. In addition, it incorporates exercises and games that stimulate the desired behavior. Remember that the key is to establish a relationship of trust and respect with your furry companion. Keep going on this journey of mutual learning!

To complete the reinforcement of your pet's long-term training, it's crucial to maintain constant communication and to reinforce desired behaviors consistently. Next, we'll explore some additional strategies to help you strengthen your furry companion's learning.

One of the most effective techniques for consolidating training is generalization. This involves teaching your pet to replicate learned behaviors in different situations and environments. For example, you can practice training in different rooms of the house or even in public places such as parks or squares. By exposing your pet to different situations, you'll be helping to reinforce their learning and ensuring that they can respond appropriately in any context.

In addition to generalization, it's important to continue reinforcing your pet's desired behaviors on a regular basis. We must not forget that learning is a continuous process and that animals need constant reinforcement to maintain their abilities. You can set up regular review sessions where you reinforce basic commands, such as "do your needs" or "go to your designated area". This will help keep learning fresh and consolidate appropriate behaviors.

Attention to your pet's signs and needs is also essential to reinforce their long-term training. Watch their behavior closely and learn to identify the signs that they need to go to the bathroom. These can include sniffing the floor, going around in circles, or agitating restlessly. The more attentive you are to your pet's needs, the easier it will be to guide them to their designated area and reinforce their learning.

Sometimes, you might encounter challenges in the long-term reinforcement process. Your pet may experience difficulties due to external factors or changes in its environment. If this happens, it's important to stay calm and resume training early on if necessary. Remember that positive reinforcement and patience are essential to overcome obstacles and help your pet maintain their abilities.

Also, at this stage of long-term reinforcement, it's important to pay attention to your pet's health and well-being. Make sure he gets a good diet, adequate exercise, and regular veterinary care. A healthy and happy pet will be more receptive to training and will be better prepared to maintain their abilities over the long term.

In short, to reinforce your pet's long-term training, you need to apply strategies such as generalization, regular review sessions, be attentive to your pet's signs and maintain their physical and emotional well-being. Every pet is unique and may respond differently to training reinforcement. Keep watching and adapting your techniques to the needs and preferences of your furry companion.

Remember that the main objective is to establish a relationship of trust and respect with your pet as you continue on this journey of mutual learning. Continue to practice and reinforce desired behaviors consistently and peacefully. Congratulations on your dedication to training your pet and enjoy the fruits of your work together!

Chapter 14: Training in Different Environments and Situations

Learn to teach your pet to urinate and defecate in different environments and situations without resorting to violence.

When we train our pets to learn to urinate and defecate properly, it's essential to teach them to do so in different environments and situations. This will allow them to adapt to different circumstances and maintain appropriate behavior no matter where they are.

One of the first steps to achieve this is to familiarize your pet with different spaces. You can start at home, in your garden, or in a space designated for them. Once they feel comfortable and have understood where they need to relieve themselves, we can move on to the next phase: teaching them to urinate and defecate outside their usual environment.

Start by taking your pet to areas outside, but close to your home, such as parks or community gardens. Make sure you choose quiet and safe places to avoid distractions that could hinder their learning. It's important for your pet to become familiar with new smells and stimuli, but without feeling overwhelmed.

During this stage, keep close control over your pet. Use a strap or harness to make sure it stays close to you and doesn't stray too far away. Establish a regular schedule to get her to relieve herself and give her enough time to do so. Remember to reward her when she does it properly, using positive reinforcements such as caresses or treats.

As your pet gets used to new environments, you may encounter challenging situations. For example, there may be loud noises or activities that get your attention and make it difficult for you to concentrate. Don't worry, it's normal and part of the learning process. Use your patience and calm to guide her in these situations and help her stay focused on the task at hand.

It's important to remember that you should never resort to violence as a form of training. Shouting, hitting or punishing your pet will not only create fear and stress, but it will also negatively affect their learning. Instead, opt for patience, consistency, and consistency.

Once your pet has adapted to different environments close to your home, it's time to take it a step further. You can start taking her to busier places, such as busy streets, busy parks, or squares. This phase will require a higher level of concentration on the part of your pet, as they will have to face more distractions and stimuli.

Remember to always maintain a positive attitude and adequately reinforce each achievement of your pet. As you get used to new environments and situations, a stronger bond will be established between you and communication will be more effective.

Training in different environments and situations is a crucial part of your pet's education process. Not only will it allow you to adapt to different circumstances, but it will also strengthen your ability to learn and obey basic commands. Remember that each pet is unique and may require different adaptation times, so patience and respect will be key in this process.

(Please note that this is the end of the first half of the chapter and no conclusion or summary is provided as per the given instructions.) Once your pet has become accustomed to busier places and has acquired the ability to maintain concentration in the face of distractions and external stimuli, it's time to continue training in different situations. This will help strengthen your skills and ensure that you can urinate and defecate properly no matter the circumstances.

One of the situations we must address is training in enclosed spaces, such as apartments or houses without a garden. There may not always be immediate access to an outside area, so it's important to teach your pet to use a designated place inside the home. Set up a specific area, such as a cat litter box or a dog grass tray, and guide your pet to use that place when they can't go outside. Remember to reward and praise her when she does it correctly, to reinforce her learning.

Another situation to consider is when you are traveling or going for a walk with your pet. During these times, it is essential that your pet knows how to adapt to different environments and continue to relieve themselves properly. Always carry essential items, such as garbage bags or a portable tray, to ensure that your pet can properly relieve itself anywhere.

For longer trips, such as vacations or moving, it's important to prepare your pet in advance to adapt to the changes. If you're traveling in a vehicle, get your pet used to being comfortable in the car through small walks and rewards. Check with your vet about your pet's needs during the trip, such as frequent stops to relieve himself and avoid digestive distress.

Also, be sure to bring your pet's familiar objects, such as their bed or toys, to help them feel safe and in a familiar environment. Establish routines similar to those you have at home for the schedule of her needs and make sure you provide adequate times for her to perform them.

Training in different environments and situations also involves teaching your pet to relieve themselves in public spaces, such as on the sidewalk during a walk. This can be a challenge, as your pet must learn to do it properly without scaring or bothering other people. Make sure you collect your pet's waste responsibly and always have bags handy for these purposes.

Remember that training is not only about teaching your pet to relieve themselves in specific places, but also about strengthening the bond between you and promoting a relationship of trust. As you progress through training, continue to reinforce your pet's positive behavior and provide him with praise and rewards when he does it properly.

In short, training in different environments and situations is essential to teach your pet to urinate and defecate without violence. From training her in closed spaces to preparing her for trips or walks, every situation represents an opportunity to strengthen her ability to adapt and learn. Remember that patience and consistency are key to successful training your pet, and always opt for positive reinforcement rather than violence. Continue to cultivate a relationship of mutual respect and enjoy every step of the educational process with your beloved pet.

Chapter 15: Using Prizes and Rewards Correctly

Explore how to effectively use rewards and rewards during training to keep your pet motivated.

The education of our pets is a task that requires patience and dedication. Among the different tools we can use to teach them effectively, prizes and rewards stand out as a very effective strategy, as long as they are used in the right way.

First of all, it's important to understand that prizes and rewards should not be used as bribes to get our pet to do what we want. They should be used as a way to positively reinforce those desirable behaviors that are going to be taught during the training process.

To use rewards effectively, it's key to identify what motivates your pet the most. Some dogs may be strongly motivated by food, while others prefer verbal praise or games. Observe your pet and determine what they like best, and that will be the best reward you can offer during training.

Once you've determined what the most effective reward will be, you need to be clear about how and when to use it. It's important to associate the reward directly with the desired behavior. For example, if you're training your dog to sit, immediately after he does it properly, you should reward him. This will help your pet understand that receiving the reward is directly linked to their positive behavior.

However, it is essential to note that rewards must be used gradually. At the beginning of training, it is advisable to reward even the small advances your pet achieves. As training progresses and behaviors become more consistent, you can gradually decrease the use of rewards, until your pet can perform the desired actions without the need for external reward.

It's important to mention that not all pets respond in the same way to prizes and rewards. Some may be highly motivated by them, while others may be more indifferent. If you notice that your pet doesn't show interest in receiving rewards, don't be discouraged. This simply means that you should look for a reward that is more valuable to her, whether it's a favorite toy or praise.

Remember that the use of rewards and rewards during training is intended to promote education based on positive reinforcement. This means that instead of punishing unwanted behavior, we seek to highlight and reward the right behaviors. In this way, we create a positive and motivating learning environment for our pets.

In short, prizes and rewards are an effective tool to keep our pet motivated during training. It is important to identify what motivates our pet the most and to use the reward immediately and consistently. Remember that the use of prizes and rewards must be gradual, decreasing their use as the pet acquires the desired behaviors. Follow these tips and you'll be on the right path to educating your pet effectively and without resorting to violence.

To be continued... Once you've established the right reward and understood the importance of using it gradually, it's time to address certain situations that may arise during the training process. Next, we'll explore some additional tips for using prizes and rewards correctly.

First, it's critical to be consistent in delivering rewards. This means that you must be fair and consistent when it comes to rewarding your pet. Whenever he performs the desired behavior, be sure to reward him in the same way, regardless of the circumstances or your mood. This will help your pet to clearly understand what is expected of them and what behaviors are rewarded.

In addition, it is important to keep in mind that rewards must not only be given during formal training, but also in everyday moments of living with your pet. For example, if your dog sits down when you ask him to do so while you prepare his food, don't hesitate to reward him for his good behavior. This reinforces the idea that desirable behaviors are valued at any time and not just during training sessions.

Another key aspect to consider is the duration and frequency of rewards. At the beginning of the training process, it is advisable to offer rewards more frequently and consistently, to motivate your pet to continue learning. Over time, as behaviors become more consistent, you can gradually space out rewards. This allows your pet to get used to performing the desired actions without relying completely on external reward.

It is important to mention that, although the use of prizes and rewards is very effective, it should not be the only tool used in training your pet. It is essential to combine it with other educational techniques, such as verbal reinforcement and the use of visual cues. This allows for more complete training and helps your pet understand the different forms of communication during the learning process.

Finally, you must remember that every pet is unique and may respond differently to prizes and rewards. Some may be extremely motivated by food, while others may prefer praise or petting. It's important to adapt the type of reward to your pet's individual preferences to keep them motivated and engaged with the training process.

In conclusion, the proper use of rewards and rewards during your pet's training is critical to maintaining motivation and encouraging desirable behaviors. Remember to be consistent in the delivery of rewards, use them both during training and in daily coexistence, adjust their duration and frequency as your pet progresses in its learning, and combine them with other education techniques. Adapting to your pet's individual preferences and treating each interaction as a learning opportunity will cement their progress. Follow these tips and you'll be on the right path to educating your pet effectively and without resorting to violence!

Chapter 16: Understanding Health Problems and Their Impact on Training

Learn about potential health problems that can affect training and how to properly address them.

When you decide to give a pet a home, you take responsibility for caring for them and ensuring their well-being in all aspects of their lives. A fundamental part of this care is to educate your pet to behave properly at home and respond to your instructions. However, it's important to understand that there are certain health problems that can directly affect training and hinder the process.

One of the most common health problems that can interfere with your pet's training is urinary tract infections. These infections can cause pain and discomfort for your pet, which will naturally affect their ability to learn and obey your instructions. If you notice that your pet has symptoms such as a frequent need to urinate, difficulty doing so or the presence of blood in the urine, it is essential that you immediately take him to the vet. Proper treatment for urinary tract infections will allow your pet to recover and resume training more effectively.

Another health problem that can negatively impact training is the presence of intestinal parasites. Often, dogs and cats can acquire worms or other types of parasites through ingestion of contaminated food or water. These parasites can cause digestive discomfort, such as diarrhea or vomiting, which will greatly hinder your ability to learn new commands or hygiene habits. If you notice signs of parasite infestation in your pet, you should go to the vet for a proper diagnosis and follow the appropriate treatment.

In addition to urinary tract infections and intestinal parasites, other health problems such as allergies, dermatological problems or chronic diseases can affect your pet's performance during the training process. It's crucial that you pay attention to any changes in your animal's behavior or health and see a veterinarian for any warning signs. Timely and adequate treatment will not only improve your pet's quality of life, but it will also facilitate their ability to learn and obey your instructions.

Remember that training your pet is a gradual process and requires patience, consistency and love. However, understanding the potential health problems that may arise during this process will allow you to address them appropriately and ensure that your pet receives the necessary care to overcome any obstacles.

As we move through the second part of this chapter, we'll explore each of the above health issues in more detail and provide you with specific strategies to effectively address them. It is essential to understand that a healthy and happy pet will be much more receptive to training and will be in optimal conditions to learn and grow with you.

Read on to find out how to overcome these obstacles and achieve a successful education for your pet!

Alcohol is extremely dangerous to pets, and even small amounts can cause severe poisoning. When ingested, alcohol can affect your pet's blood sugar levels, leading to dangerously low levels or even coma. It can also cause vomiting, diarrhea, difficulty breathing, seizures, and in severe cases, death.

Another common household item that can be toxic to pets is chocolate. While most people know that chocolate is harmful to dogs, it can also be toxic to cats. Chocolate contains theobromine and caffeine, which are both stimulants that can affect your pet's heart, central nervous system, and gastrointestinal tract. The effects of chocolate poisoning in pets can range from mild symptoms such as restlessness, increased heart rate, and vomiting, to more serious symptoms like tremors, seizures, and even death.

It's important to keep all medications, both prescription and over-the-counter, out of your pet's reach. Many human medications are toxic to pets, even in small doses. Painkillers like ibuprofen and acetaminophen, for example, can cause severe kidney or liver damage in pets. Antidepressants, blood pressure medications, and sleep aids can also be toxic to your furry friends.

Certain foods that are safe for humans can be toxic to pets. Onions and garlic, for instance, contain compounds that can cause damage to your pet's red blood cells, leading to anemia. Grapes and raisins are also highly toxic to dogs and can cause kidney failure. Other foods to avoid giving your pets include avocados, alcohol, caffeine, and anything sweetened with xylitol, such as gum or baked goods.

Plants can also pose a risk to your pet's health if ingested. Lilies, for example, are highly toxic to cats and can cause kidney failure. Other common plants that are toxic to pets include tulips, azaleas, sago palms, and daffodils. It's important to research the plants in and around your home to ensure they are safe for your furry friend.

If you suspect that your pet has ingested something toxic, it's important to act quickly. Contact your veterinarian or an animal poison control center immediately for guidance. They can provide you with specific instructions on how to induce vomiting or administer activated charcoal, depending on the situation.

Prevention is key when it comes to keeping your pets safe from toxic substances. Be mindful of what you keep in your home and ensure that potentially dangerous items are securely stored out of your pet's reach. It's also a good idea to remove any toxic plants from your home or garden.

In conclusion, it's essential to be aware of potential hazards in your home that can be toxic to your pets. From household chemicals to human medications and certain foods, there are many substances that can pose a risk to your furry friend's health. By educating yourself and taking preventative measures, you can help keep your pet safe and ensure a happy and healthy life for them. Remember, your pet's well-being is in your hands.

Chapter 17: The Role of Owners in Successful Training

Understand how your role as an owner influences training success and how to develop a trusting relationship with your pet.

Training a pet is a crucial task for its proper development and coexistence. However, it's not just about teaching him to urinate and defecate in the right place, but about establishing effective communication and a trusting relationship between you and your furry companion. In this chapter, we'll delve into the critical role that owners play in the successful training of their pets and how they can develop a healthy and lasting relationship.

First, it is essential to understand that dogs and cats are beings with needs and behaviors specific to their species. Everyone has their own temperament and personality, which can influence their ability to learn and adapt. Therefore, it is essential that you familiarize yourself with the characteristics of your pet and take them into account during the training process.

In addition, it is essential that you take the time necessary to establish a routine with your pet. Consistency is key to their learning, and that means setting fixed times for their walks, eating and playing time. By maintaining a stable routine, you provide your pet with a sense of security and predictability, making it easier to train.

Another fundamental aspect is the use of positive reinforcements during training. Violence or physical punishment should never be used as training methods, as they only create fear and stress in your pet. Instead, it praises and rewards their desirable behaviors with cuddles, prizes, or kind words. This way, you'll associate the learning process with positive experiences and be more motivated to keep learning.

It's also important to remember that training shouldn't be limited to just when you want to teach him to urinate and defecate in a specific place. You must encourage education in all aspects of their life, from teaching them to walk properly on a leash to behaving appropriately in social situations. This will help strengthen his bond with you and help him become a balanced member of the family.

However, it is essential to understand that each pet has its own learning rate and that not all dogs or cats will be trained in the same way. Some can learn quickly, while others will require more time and patience. In this sense, it's essential that your arm yourself with patience and don't get frustrated if progress is slow. Remember that training is a gradual process that requires perseverance and dedication.

In this first part of the chapter, we explored some key aspects of the role of owners in successfully training their pets. We have understood the importance of knowing the individual characteristics of our pet, establishing routines, using positive reinforcement and encouraging education in all aspects of their lives.

In the second part of this chapter, we'll discuss specific strategies for teaching your pet to urinate and defecate without resorting to violence. We'll explore positive reinforcement techniques, implementing clear schedules and signals, and the importance of patience and consistency in the process. Get ready to discover how you can become an effective trainer and establish a relationship based on trust and respect with your pet.

Continued... In this second part of the chapter, we will focus on practical and effective strategies to teach your pet to urinate and defecate without resorting to violence. Using positive reinforcement and consistency, you'll achieve optimal results and further strengthen your relationship with your furry companion.

One of the keys to successful training is to establish a clear and consistent signal to tell your pet that it's the right time to relieve themselves. For example, you can choose a word like "do" or "bathroom" and use it every time you take it to the designated area. This way, your pet will associate the word with the action and understand what is expected of it.

Patience is critical during this process, especially if your pet isn't showing immediate progress. Remember that each animal has its own learning rate and some may need more time than others to understand what is being asked of them. Avoid scolding or punishing your pet if it makes a mistake, as this will only lead to confusion and stress. Instead, use positive reinforcement to reward and praise when you relieve yourself in the right place.

Another important aspect is the use of rewards as an incentive for your pet during training. The prizes can be small snacks or toys that your pet likes. When he succeeds in relieving himself in the right place, warmly congratulate him and give him the prize right away. This will reinforce the positive association and motivate your pet to repeat the desired behavior in the future.

It is essential to establish a regular routine so that your pet gets used to relieving himself at specific times of the day. Take it to the designated place after waking up, after eating and before sleeping. If your pet is unable to relieve himself at that time, you can try again after a certain time. Consistent schedules will help your pet to establish the desired pattern and to associate the right time with the right place.

Also remember the importance of keeping the designated place clean and free of unpleasant odors. If your pet notices a strong smell of urine or feces in the place, it is likely that they will use it again. Clean the area with products that eliminate odors and avoid scolding your pet if it breaks the rules again. Patience and consistency will be your best allies during this process.

In addition to home training, it is also advisable to take your pet for regular walks so that they can relieve themselves away from home. This will help you socialize, exercise, and maintain adequate physical and mental health. Take him to specific areas where he can feel comfortable and relaxed to relieve himself.

In conclusion, the role of owners in successfully training their pets is crucial. By knowing your pet's individual characteristics, establishing routines, using positive reinforcement and patience, you can teach your pet to urinate and defecate without resorting to violence. Remember that training is a gradual process and requires perseverance and dedication. Get ready to enjoy a harmonious and respectful relationship with your furry companion!

Chapter 18: Useful training tools and accessories

The process of training a pet can be a challenging task, but it can also be a rewarding experience for both the owner and the animal. However, it is important to ensure that this process takes place without resorting to violence. There are a wide variety of tools and accessories that can be useful during your pet's training. Next, we'll explore some of them.

1. Training straps: Training straps are essential tools for teaching your pet to walk properly next to you. These straps are designed to provide additional control and allow for greater comfort during walks. In addition, some training straps have additional handles that allow for better grip in situations where greater control is needed.

2. Training Clicker: The training clicker is a small, portable device that produces a distinctive sound when pressed. This tool is used to mark the desired behavior and to reinforce it positively. By combining the sound of the clicker with a reward, such as a treat, your pet will associate the sound with correct behavior.

3. Anti-pull collars: Anti-pull collars are useful for correcting problems with pulling the strap during walks. These collars are designed to apply mild pressure around the neck when the pet pulls excessively on the leash. However, it is essential to use them correctly and without applying excessive force, as their goal is to avoid discomfort, not to cause harm.

4. Interactive toys: Interactive toys are great tools to keep your pet entertained and mentally stimulated. These toys usually contain hidden

prizes or challenges that require the pet to solve them to get the reward. This helps to channel your energy in a positive way and to avoid destructive behavior.

5. Training barriers: If you want to delimit certain areas of your home where your pet should not enter, training barriers are an excellent option. These barriers can be doors or fences that are easily installed and are adjustable according to your needs. With these tools, you can keep your pet away from certain rooms or areas where it can cause harm or become endangered.

6. Transport boxes: Transport boxes are essential tools for training and keeping your pet safe. These boxes provide a safe and cozy space where your pet can rest and relax. They are also useful for cleaning and sphincter control training, as they provide a specific place for your pet to relieve himself.

7. Food puzzles: Food puzzles are a great way to keep your pet busy while stimulating their mind. These toys are designed to hide small amounts of food inside them, and your pet will have to solve the puzzle to access the food. This is especially useful for dogs and cats that can easily get bored and need mental enrichment.

Remember that these tools and accessories are complementary to training, and do not replace the importance of positive reinforcement, patience and consistency. It is essential to establish a relationship of trust and respect with your pet, and to ensure that the training is carried out in a friendly manner and without resorting to any type of violence.

In the next part of this chapter, we'll explore other tools and accessories that may be beneficial for training your pet. Don't miss it, it will be a surprise that will help you strengthen your relationship with your faithful companion! 8. Self-dispensing water bowls: Self-dispensing water bowls are very useful tools to ensure that your pet always has fresh, clean water available. These bowls have a water tank connected to a dispensing system that is activated when the water level drops. This is especially useful if you have to be away from home for long periods of time or if you have several pets that share the same water bowl.

9. GPS collars: GPS collars are an excellent choice if you want to keep your pet safe and in control. These collars are equipped with a tracking device that allows you to locate your pet in real time through a mobile application. This can be especially useful if your pet tends to run away or if you enjoy outdoor activities where it can easily get lost.

10. Pet seat belts: If you're traveling with your pet in the car, it's important to ensure their safety. Seat belts designed specifically for pets are an excellent option to keep your travel companion safe while traveling. These belts fit your pet's harness and connect to the car's seat belt, preventing your pet from moving freely around the vehicle.

11. Brush and comb set: Taking care of your pet's coat is essential to keeping it healthy and clean. A set of brushes and combs suitable for your pet's hair type can help keep their fur untangled and free of knots. In addition, regular brushing is also a great way to strengthen the bond with your pet and provide them with moments of relaxation.

12. Padded beds and blankets: To ensure your pet's rest and comfort, it's important to provide them with a padded bed or blanket. These accessories will provide you with a safe and comforting place where you can relax and sleep peacefully. In addition, having your own bed or blanket can also help prevent your pet from lying on furniture or in your bed.

13. Programmable food dispensers: If you have busy schedules or if you want to control the amount of food your pet consumes, a programmable food dispenser can be of great help. These devices allow you to program how much and when you want food to be served to your pet. This is especially useful for controlling the feeding of pets with specific dietary needs or if your pet tends to overfeed.

14. Bite repellents: If your pet tends to bite inappropriate objects or has destructive behaviors, bite repellents can be an effective solution. These repellents are designed to emit an unpleasant smell or taste for

your pet, deterring it from biting or damaging objects. Remember that it is important to use repellents that are safe for your pet and that do not cause any harm.

Remember that the selection of tools and accessories will depend on your pet's specific needs and lifestyle. Make sure you carefully research and select the products that best suit your needs and those of your pet. Never forget that training should be a positive and respectful experience, based on positive reinforcement and patience.

Congratulations! You've explored a variety of useful tools and accessories that can make it easier for you to train your pet without resorting to violence. Now you're ready to put these tips into practice and strengthen your relationship with your faithful companion. In the next chapter, we'll discover how to establish an effective training routine and how to address some common challenges you may encounter along the way. Don't miss it!

Chapter 19: Solving Recurring Disposal Problems

Learn to identify and resolve recurring elimination problems in your pet using positive training methods.

The education of our pets is a responsibility that we must take seriously. One of the fundamental aspects of this work is to teach them to relieve themselves properly, preventing recurring elimination problems from occurring. Fortunately, there are positive training methods that allow us to effectively address this situation.

The first step in solving recurring elimination problems is to identify the underlying causes. These problems can be caused by various reasons, such as the lack of adequate education from an early age, changes in the pet's environment, health problems or stressful situations. It's important to note that violence should never be used as a means to correct these behaviors.

Once we've identified the cause of the problem, it's time to implement positive training methods. These methods are based on rewarding desired behaviors rather than punishing unwanted ones. It's essential to remember that our pets learn best through motivation and positive reinforcement.

An effective strategy to teach our pet to urinate and defecate in the right place is to use positive reinforcement at the right time. When you notice that your pet is about to relieve himself in the right place, congratulate him and reward him with cuddles, words of encouragement, or even his favorite treat. This will help to reinforce the association between the desired behavior and the positive stimulus.

It is also important to establish a feeding and walking routine for our pet. This will provide you with a regular schedule for your physiological needs and facilitate your learning. Feeding your pet at the same time every day and taking them out for a walk after each meal will allow their body to get used to a set pattern, thus avoiding recurring elimination problems.

Accidents can occur during the training process, but it's essential to stay calm and avoid any negative reactions. We should never punish or scold our pet for relieving themselves in the wrong place, as this will only create confusion and fear in it. If you surprise your pet on the spot, simply take it quietly and safely to the right place and praise it when it ends up there.

Remember that every pet is unique and may require a personalized approach to their training. Observe your furry companion's behaviors, be patient, and be consistent in your teaching. If recurring elimination problems persist despite your efforts, it is advisable to seek the advice of an animal behavior expert, such as a veterinarian or professional trainer.

In conclusion, solving your pet's recurring elimination problems is possible using positive training methods. Identifying underlying causes, establishing routines, and positively reinforcing desired behaviors are key tools in this process. Remember that patience and consistency are essential. With time and dedication, you'll help your pet learn to relieve himself in the right place without resorting to violence.

End of the first chapter.

Remember that the next chapter will address advanced techniques for solving more complex removal problems. Don't miss it! Once we have established a solid foundation in training our pet to learn to relieve itself in the right place, we can use more advanced techniques to solve more complex recurring elimination problems. Below, we'll introduce you to some additional strategies that may be useful in these cases.

An effective technique for correcting unwanted behavior is the use of negative reinforcement. This involves the elimination of an aversive stimulus when our pet performs the wrong behavior. For example, if your dog is used to relieving himself inside the house and you catch him in the act, you can make a loud and unpleasant sound, such as a loud applause or a knock on the door, to interrupt him. Then quickly get him to the right place and praise him when he's done there. The objective of this technique is to associate unwanted behavior with a negative consequence and to motivate our pet to avoid repeating it.

Another strategy is to use the confinement technique when you can't directly monitor your pet. Confinement involves keeping your pet in a designated area, such as a playpen or a small room with closed doors, when you can't be there to monitor them. Make sure you provide him with a comfortable area with his favorite toys and accessories, as well as his proper place to relieve himself. This will help prevent accidents and reinforce the habit of relieving yourself in the right place.

It's important to remember that the process of educating a pet requires time and patience. Each animal is unique and will learn at its own pace. Keep your training techniques consistent and avoid constantly changing them, as this can cause confusion for your pet.

If recurring elimination problems persist despite your efforts, it is advisable to seek the advice of an animal behavior expert. A veterinarian or professional trainer will be able to assess the situation and provide you with a personalized approach to solving your pet's specific problems.

In conclusion, learning to solve recurring elimination problems in our pet requires an approach based on positive training methods and patience. Identifying the underlying causes, establishing routines, using positive and negative reinforcements, as well as confinement, can be effective strategies in this process. Remember that keeping calm and avoiding any form of violence are essential for the well-being and learning of our pet.

Continue to dedicate time and effort to educating your pet, and over time, you'll help them learn to relieve themselves properly. The next chapter will explore techniques to address other common problems in pet education. Don't miss it!

Chapter 20: Maintaining Continuing Education

Discover the importance of continuous learning and how to maintain effective education for your pet over time.

As your pet develops and grows with you, it's essential to understand that education should not be a static, time-limited process. Like humans, animals also need to constantly learn and grow to adapt to different situations and environments. Maintaining continuous education for your pet is essential to their development and overall well-being.

One of the most important aspects of continuous learning is the ability to adapt. As with humans, pets' needs and behaviors can change as they grow and face new experiences. For example, a puppy that learned to urinate on newspaper inside the house when he was young will need to learn to do so outside as he grows up. It's critical to be willing to adapt teaching techniques to ensure effective education at every stage of your pet's life.

In addition, continuous learning promotes a stronger bond between you and your pet. Through dedication and constant interaction, you can continue to develop a relationship based on trust and mutual respect. By actively engaging in your pet's education over time, you'll be showing them that you care and that you're committed to their well-being. This will strengthen the emotional bond between the two and facilitate effective communication.

An effective way to maintain continuing education is to establish consistent routines and habits. Animals are creatures of habit, so establishing a structure in their daily lives provides them with security and makes it easier for them to learn. For example, if you want your pet to learn to urinate in a specific place, it's crucial to establish regular walking times and reward their proper behavior. This will give them clear direction and allow them to understand what is expected of them.

Consistency is also key to continuing education. It's not just about teaching your pet once and hoping they'll remember it forever. You need to be persistent and patient, constantly reinforcing the desired behavioral patterns. Devoting time and effort to educating your pet on an ongoing basis will ensure positive long-term results.

Remember that continuing education not only involves teaching new tricks or behaviors, but also reinforcing and maintaining those you have already learned. Your pet may forget certain commands or habits if they are not regularly reminded. Therefore, it is essential to keep practicing and reviewing the lessons learned to ensure that they stay present in your mind.

In short, maintaining continuous education for your pet is essential for their development and well-being. Adapting to their changing needs, establishing consistent routines and habits, and being consistent in reinforcing desired behaviors are the pillars of effective continuous learning. By maintaining a consistent and dedicated education, you'll establish a stronger bond with your pet and provide them with the tools they need to adapt to different situations throughout their lives.

>>> Thriller... It will continue in the next chapter. To maintain continuous and effective education for your pet over time, it's important to consider a few key aspects. First, it's essential to keep practicing and reviewing the lessons learned to ensure that they stay present in your mind. Your pet may forget certain commands or habits if they aren't reminded regularly, so repetition is essential.

In addition, you must be consistent in reinforcing desired behaviors. By rewarding and praising your pet for their good behavior, you will be teaching them what you expect from them and you will positively reinforce their learning. Remember that rewards can vary; some animals may like to receive caresses or verbal praise, while others may be more motivated by a material reward, such as a treat. Observe the most appropriate response for your pet and use it as motivation for their learning.

Another strategy is to establish clear limits and rules in living with your pet. This involves establishing what behaviors are acceptable and which are not. When your pet behaves inappropriately, correct it firmly but without resorting to violence. You can use a correction word such as "no" or "loud" and accompany it with a gesture or sound that captures their attention. It's important to remember that education doesn't involve physically punishing your pet, as this will only generate fear and stress, and make it difficult for them to learn.

It's also essential to dedicate time and effort to educating your pet on an ongoing basis. It's not just about teaching him once and hoping he'll remember it forever. Animals, like human beings, need practice and repetition to consolidate their learning. Spend at least a few minutes a day working on basic commands such as sitting, staying, or coming when called.

Another important aspect of continuing education is the socialization of your pet. Exposing her to different people, animals and environments from an early age will help her better adapt to new and unknown situations. Organize walks and encounters with other trusted dogs or animals, and allow them to interact with other people. In this way, your pet will learn to behave appropriately in different contexts and will be more sociable and friendly.

Finally, remember that every pet is unique and has its own needs and pace of learning. When maintaining continuing education, it's important to be patient and adapt to your level of understanding. Some animals can learn quickly, while others may require more time and practice. Be patient and positively reinforce every small advance you notice in your pet.

In conclusion, maintaining continuous education for your pet is essential for their development and well-being throughout their lives. To achieve this, it's important to remember the importance of repetition and constant reinforcement, to establish clear limits and rules, to dedicate time and effort to training, to socialize your pet and to be patient and adapt to their individual needs. By following these tips, you'll be building a relationship based on trust and mutual respect, and providing your pet with the tools they need to adapt to different situations in their lives.

Disclaimer

The information provided in this book is for general informational and educational purposes only. The author and publisher make no representation or warranties with respect to the accuracy, applicability, fitness, or completeness of the contents of this book. They are not intended to be a substitute for professional advice, diagnosis, or treatment. The author and publisher shall not be held liable for any loss or damage allegedly arising from any information or suggestions within this book.

By reading this book, you agree that you are solely responsible for your own decisions and actions. If you require specific advice for your personal situation, consult with a qualified professional.

The views expressed by the author do not necessarily reflect the views of the publisher. All information is provided on an as-is basis.

Don't miss out!

Visit the website below and you can sign up to receive emails whenever Gonzalo Estrada publishes a new book. There's no charge and no obligation.

https://books2read.com/r/B-A-OZBBB-UHEZC

Also by Gonzalo Estrada

Self Healing
Visualiza tu Éxito
Cultivando Líderes
Afirmaciones y Empoderamiento
Semillas de Cambio
Cómo convertir TikTok en una máquina de hacer dinero
Cómo hacer dinero con Pinterest
Cómo hacer un ensayo
Cómo Pedir un Aumento de Sueldo
Currículo Poderoso
Entrenamiento sin Violencia
Entrevista Laboral
Gana Dinero con X (Twitter)
Ganar Masa Muscular
Volver a Empezar; el arte de reinventarse
Analiza Resuelve Ejecuta
Aromatherapy, The natural path to your pet´s well being
Holistic Feeding
The ABC of Educating Your Pet
The Art of Cosmic Connection
The Art of Feng Shui applied to your Pets
From Scarcity to Abundance
The English Bulldog in The Family
The French Bulldog
Therapeutic Massages for Pets

Pets and Crystal Therapy
The Maltese Bichon
Transform Your Problems into Opportunities
Esto ya Cambió
Cómo crear Prompts de forma correcta.